Alfred's
Lesson Assignment
for Piano Students

MW01097447

Contents

My Name is:

_____

My Teacher's Name is:

_____

My Address is:

_____

_____

My Teacher's Address is:

_____

_____

My Phone Number is:

_____

My Teacher's Phone Number is:

_____

Alfred

Assignment
For Next Lesson

| Date |
| Day |
| Time |

Today's Lesson
Date

Day

Time

Method Books	New pages	Review pages
☐ Lesson Book		
☐ Theory Book		
☐ Recital/Solo Book		
☐		
☐		
Supplementary Solo, Duet & Ensemble Books		
☐		
☐		
☐		
Sheet Music Solos, Duets & Ensembles		
☐		
☐		
☐		

A check in the box is a reminder to read the Practice Suggestions on the next page.

Daily Practice Time
(in minutes)

Monday _____

Tuesday _____

Wednesday _____

Thursday _____

Friday _____

Saturday _____

Sunday _____

Practice Tips
What to watch during practice sessions this week:

☐ Dynamics

☐ Fingering

☐ Hand Position

☐ Rhythm

☐ Other_____

Teacher's Evaluation of Lesson
☐ Excellent   ☐ Very Good   ☐ Good   ☐ Satisfactory   ☐ Needs Attention

Comments:

Note from Teacher to Parent:

Note from Parent to Teacher:

What to Bring to the Next Lesson: In addition to all the music listed in the Assignment section above, bring the following materials to the next lesson:

Practice Suggestions

Assignment
For Next Lesson

Date
Day
Time

Today's Lesson
Date
_____
Day
_____
Time
_____

Method Books	New pages	Review pages
☐ Lesson Book		
☐ Theory Book		
☐ Recital/Solo Book		
☐		
☐		
Supplementary Solo, Duet & Ensemble Books		
☐		
☐		
☐		
Sheet Music Solos, Duets & Ensembles		
☐		
☐		
☐		

A check in the box is a reminder to read the Practice Suggestions on the next page.

Daily Practice Time
(in minutes)

Monday _____
Tuesday _____
Wednesday _____
Thursday _____
Friday _____
Saturday _____
Sunday _____

Practice Tips
What to watch during practice sessions this week:

☐ Dynamics
☐ Fingering
☐ Hand Position
☐ Rhythm
☐ Other _____
_____

Teacher's Evaluation of Lesson

☐ Excellent　　☐ Very Good　　☐ Good　　☐ Satisfactory　　☐ Needs Attention

Comments:
....
....

Note from Teacher to Parent:

Note from Parent to Teacher:

What to Bring to the Next Lesson: In addition to all the music listed in the Assignment section above, bring the following materials to the next lesson:
....
....

Practice Suggestions

Assignment
For Next Lesson

Date	
Day	
Time	

Today's Lesson

Date _____

Day _____

Time _____

Method Books	New pages	Review pages
☐ Lesson Book		
☐ Theory Book		
☐ Recital/Solo Book		
☐		
☐		
Supplementary Solo, Duet & Ensemble Books		
☐		
☐		
☐		
Sheet Music Solos, Duets & Ensembles		
☐		
☐		
☐		

A check in the box is a reminder to read the Practice Suggestions on the next page.

Daily Practice Time
(in minutes)

Monday _____

Tuesday _____

Wednesday _____

Thursday _____

Friday _____

Saturday _____

Sunday _____

Practice Tips

What to watch during practice sessions this week:

☐ Dynamics

☐ Fingering

☐ Hand Position

☐ Rhythm

☐ Other _____

_____

Teacher's Evaluation of Lesson

☐ Excellent   ☐ Very Good   ☐ Good   ☐ Satisfactory   ☐ Needs Attention

Comments: ....

....

Note from Teacher to Parent:

....

....

....

....

Note from Parent to Teacher:

....

....

....

....

What to Bring to the Next Lesson: In addition to all the music listed in the Assignment section above, bring the following materials to the next lesson: ....

....

6

Practice Suggestions

Assignment
For Next Lesson

Date
Day
Time

Today's Lesson
Date _____

Day _____

Time _____

Method Books	New pages	Review pages
☐ Lesson Book		
☐ Theory Book		
☐ Recital/Solo Book		
☐		
☐		
Supplementary Solo, Duet & Ensemble Books		
☐		
☐		
☐		
Sheet Music Solos, Duets & Ensembles		
☐		
☐		
☐		

A check in the box is a reminder to read the Practice Suggestions on the next page.

Daily Practice Time
(in minutes)

Monday _____

Tuesday _____

Wednesday _____

Thursday _____

Friday _____

Saturday _____

Sunday _____

Practice Tips
What to watch during practice sessions this week:

☐ Dynamics

☐ Fingering

☐ Hand Position

☐ Rhythm

☐ Other_____

Teacher's Evaluation of Lesson
☐ Excellent   ☐ Very Good   ☐ Good   ☐ Satisfactory   ☐ Needs Attention

Comments: ....

....

....

Note from Teacher to Parent:

Note from Parent to Teacher:

What to Bring to the Next Lesson: In addition to all the music listed in the Assignment section above, bring the following materials to the next lesson:

Practice Suggestions

Assignment

For Next Lesson

	Date
	Day
	Time

Today's Lesson

Date _____

Day _____

Time _____

Method Books	New pages	Review pages
☐ Lesson Book		
☐ Theory Book		
☐ Recital/Solo Book		
☐		
☐		
Supplementary Solo, Duet & Ensemble Books		
☐		
☐		
☐		
Sheet Music Solos, Duets & Ensembles		
☐		
☐		
☐		

A check in the box is a reminder to read the Practice Suggestions on the next page.

Daily Practice Time
(in minutes)

Monday _____

Tuesday _____

Wednesday _____

Thursday _____

Friday _____

Saturday _____

Sunday _____

Practice Tips

What to watch during practice sessions this week:

☐ Dynamics

☐ Fingering

☐ Hand Position

☐ Rhythm

☐ Other_____

_____

Teacher's Evaluation of Lesson

☐ Excellent   ☐ Very Good   ☐ Good   ☐ Satisfactory   ☐ Needs Attention

Comments: ....

....

....

Note from Teacher to Parent:

....

....

....

....

Note from Parent to Teacher:

....

....

....

....

What to Bring to the Next Lesson: In addition to all the music listed in the Assignment section above, bring the following materials to the next lesson: ....

....

Practice Suggestions

Assignment
For Next Lesson

Date	
Day	
Time	

Today's Lesson

Date _____

Day _____

Time _____

Method Books	New pages	Review pages
☐ Lesson Book		
☐ Theory Book		
☐ Recital/Solo Book		
☐		
☐		
Supplementary Solo, Duet & Ensemble Books		
☐		
☐		
☐		
Sheet Music Solos, Duets & Ensembles		
☐		
☐		
☐		

A check in the box is a reminder to read the Practice Suggestions on the next page.

Daily Practice Time
(in minutes)

Monday _____

Tuesday _____

Wednesday _____

Thursday _____

Friday _____

Saturday _____

Sunday _____

Practice Tips

What to watch during practice sessions this week:

☐ Dynamics

☐ Fingering

☐ Hand Position

☐ Rhythm

☐ Other _____

_____

Teacher's Evaluation of Lesson

☐ Excellent   ☐ Very Good   ☐ Good   ☐ Satisfactory   ☐ Needs Attention

Comments: ....

....

....

Note from Teacher to Parent:

....

....

....

....

....

Note from Parent to Teacher:

....

....

....

....

....

What to Bring to the Next Lesson: In addition to all the music listed in the Assignment section above, bring the following materials to the next lesson: ....

....

....

Practice Suggestions

Assignment
For Next Lesson

Date
Day
Time

Today's Lesson
Date _____

Day _____

Time _____

Method Books	New pages	Review pages
☐ Lesson Book		
☐ Theory Book		
☐ Recital/Solo Book		
☐		
☐		
Supplementary Solo, Duet & Ensemble Books		
☐		
☐		
☐		
Sheet Music Solos, Duets & Ensembles		
☐		
☐		
☐		

A check in the box is a reminder to read the Practice Suggestions on the next page.

Daily Practice Time
(in minutes)

Monday _____

Tuesday _____

Wednesday _____

Thursday _____

Friday _____

Saturday _____

Sunday _____

Practice Tips
What to watch during practice sessions this week:

☐ Dynamics

☐ Fingering

☐ Hand Position

☐ Rhythm

☐ Other_____

_____

Teacher's Evaluation of Lesson

☐ Excellent ☐ Very Good ☐ Good ☐ Satisfactory ☐ Needs Attention

Comments: ....

....

Note from Teacher to Parent:

Note from Parent to Teacher:

What to Bring to the Next Lesson: In addition to all the music listed in the Assignment section above, bring the following materials to the next lesson:

Practice Suggestions

Assignment
For Next Lesson

Date	
Day	
Time	

Today's Lesson

Date _____

Day _____

Time _____

Method Books	New pages	Review pages
☐ Lesson Book		
☐ Theory Book		
☐ Recital/Solo Book		
☐		
☐		
Supplementary Solo, Duet & Ensemble Books		
☐		
☐		
☐		
Sheet Music Solos, Duets & Ensembles		
☐		
☐		
☐		

A check in the box is a reminder to read the Practice Suggestions on the next page.

Daily Practice Time
(in minutes)

Monday _____

Tuesday _____

Wednesday _____

Thursday _____

Friday _____

Saturday _____

Sunday _____

Practice Tips

What to watch during practice sessions this week:

☐ Dynamics

☐ Fingering

☐ Hand Position

☐ Rhythm

☐ Other _____

_____

Teacher's Evaluation of Lesson

☐ Excellent ☐ Very Good ☐ Good ☐ Satisfactory ☐ Needs Attention

Comments: ....

....

....

Note from Teacher to Parent:

....

....

....

....

Note from Parent to Teacher:

....

....

....

....

What to Bring to the Next Lesson: In addition to all the music listed in the Assignment section above, bring the following materials to the next lesson:

....

....

Practice Suggestions

Assignment
For Next Lesson

Date	
Day	
Time	

Today's Lesson

Date _____

Day _____

Time _____

Method Books	New pages	Review pages
☐ Lesson Book		
☐ Theory Book		
☐ Recital/Solo Book		
☐		
☐		
Supplementary Solo, Duet & Ensemble Books		
☐		
☐		
☐		
Sheet Music Solos, Duets & Ensembles		
☐		
☐		
☐		

A check in the box is a reminder to read the Practice Suggestions on the next page.

Daily Practice Time
(in minutes)

Monday _____

Tuesday _____

Wednesday _____

Thursday _____

Friday _____

Saturday _____

Sunday _____

Practice Tips

What to watch during practice sessions this week:

☐ Dynamics

☐ Fingering

☐ Hand Position

☐ Rhythm

☐ Other_____

_____

Teacher's Evaluation of Lesson

☐ Excellent   ☐ Very Good   ☐ Good   ☐ Satisfactory   ☐ Needs Attention

Comments: ....

....

Note from Teacher to Parent:

....

....

....

....

....

Note from Parent to Teacher:

....

....

....

....

....

What to Bring to the Next Lesson: In addition to all the music listed in the Assignment section above, bring the following materials to the next lesson: ....

....

Practice Suggestions

Assignment
For Next Lesson

Date	
Day	
Time	

Method Books	New pages	Review pages
☐ Lesson Book		
☐ Theory Book		
☐ Recital/Solo Book		
☐		
☐		
Supplementary Solo, Duet & Ensemble Books		
☐		
☐		
☐		
Sheet Music Solos, Duets & Ensembles		
☐		
☐		
☐		

A check in the box is a reminder to read the Practice Suggestions on the next page.

Daily Practice Time
(in minutes)

Monday _____

Tuesday _____

Wednesday _____

Thursday _____

Friday _____

Saturday _____

Sunday _____

Practice Tips
What to watch during practice sessions this week:

☐ Dynamics

☐ Fingering

☐ Hand Position

☐ Rhythm

☐ Other _____

_____

Teacher's Evaluation of Lesson

☐ Excellent   ☐ Very Good   ☐ Good   ☐ Satisfactory   ☐ Needs Attention

Comments: ....

....

....

Note from Teacher to Parent:

....

....

....

....

....

....

Note from Parent to Teacher:

....

....

....

....

....

....

What to Bring to the Next Lesson: In addition to all the music listed in the Assignment section above, bring the following materials to the next lesson:

....

....

Practice Suggestions

Assignment
For Next Lesson

Date	
Day	
Time	

Method Books	New pages	Review pages
☐ Lesson Book		
☐ Theory Book		
☐ Recital/Solo Book		
☐		
☐		
Supplementary Solo, Duet & Ensemble Books		
☐		
☐		
☐		
Sheet Music Solos, Duets & Ensembles		
☐		
☐		
☐		

A check in the box is a reminder to read the Practice Suggestions on the next page.

Daily Practice Time
(in minutes)

Monday _____

Tuesday _____

Wednesday _____

Thursday _____

Friday _____

Saturday _____

Sunday _____

Practice Tips

What to watch during practice sessions this week:

☐ Dynamics

☐ Fingering

☐ Hand Position

☐ Rhythm

☐ Other _____

_____

Teacher's Evaluation of Lesson

☐ Excellent ☐ Very Good ☐ Good ☐ Satisfactory ☐ Needs Attention

Comments: ....

....

....

Note from Teacher to Parent:

....

....

....

....

Note from Parent to Teacher:

....

....

....

....

What to Bring to the Next Lesson: In addition to all the music listed in the Assignment section above, bring the following materials to the next lesson: ....

....

....

Practice Suggestions

Assignment
For Next Lesson

Date	
Day	
Time	

Method Books	New pages	Review pages
☐ Lesson Book		
☐ Theory Book		
☐ Recital/Solo Book		
☐		
☐		
Supplementary Solo, Duet & Ensemble Books		
☐		
☐		
☐		
Sheet Music Solos, Duets & Ensembles		
☐		
☐		
☐		

A check in the box is a reminder to read the Practice Suggestions on the next page.

Daily Practice Time
(in minutes)

Monday _____

Tuesday _____

Wednesday _____

Thursday _____

Friday _____

Saturday _____

Sunday _____

Practice Tips

What to watch during practice sessions this week:

☐ Dynamics

☐ Fingering

☐ Hand Position

☐ Rhythm

☐ Other_____

_____

Teacher's Evaluation of Lesson

☐ Excellent   ☐ Very Good   ☐ Good   ☐ Satisfactory   ☐ Needs Attention

Comments: ....

....

....

Note from Teacher to Parent:

....

....

....

....

....

....

Note from Parent to Teacher:

....

....

....

....

....

....

What to Bring to the Next Lesson: In addition to all the music listed in the Assignment section above, bring the following materials to the next lesson:

....

....

Practice Suggestions

Assignment
For Next Lesson

Date	
Day	
Time	

Method Books	New pages	Review pages
☐ Lesson Book		
☐ Theory Book		
☐ Recital/Solo Book		
☐		
☐		
Supplementary Solo, Duet & Ensemble Books		
☐		
☐		
☐		
Sheet Music Solos, Duets & Ensembles		
☐		
☐		
☐		

A check in the box is a reminder to read the Practice Suggestions on the next page.

Daily Practice Time
(in minutes)

Monday _____

Tuesday _____

Wednesday _____

Thursday _____

Friday _____

Saturday _____

Sunday _____

Practice Tips
What to watch during practice sessions this week:

☐ Dynamics

☐ Fingering

☐ Hand Position

☐ Rhythm

☐ Other_____

_____

Teacher's Evaluation of Lesson

☐ Excellent ☐ Very Good ☐ Good ☐ Satisfactory ☐ Needs Attention

Comments: ....

....

....

Note from Teacher to Parent:

Note from Parent to Teacher:

What to Bring to the Next Lesson: In addition to all the music listed in the Assignment section above, bring the following materials to the next lesson: ....

....

Practice Suggestions

_____
_____
_____
_____
_____

_____
_____
_____
_____
_____

_____
_____
_____
_____
_____

Assignment
For Next Lesson

Date
Day
Time

Date _____

Day _____

Time _____

Method Books	New pages	Review pages
☐ Lesson Book		
☐ Theory Book		
☐ Recital/Solo Book		
☐		
☐		
Supplementary Solo, Duet & Ensemble Books		
☐		
☐		
☐		
Sheet Music Solos, Duets & Ensembles		
☐		
☐		
☐		

A check in the box is a reminder to read the Practice Suggestions on the next page.

Daily Practice Time
(in minutes)

Monday _____

Tuesday _____

Wednesday _____

Thursday _____

Friday _____

Saturday _____

Sunday _____

Practice Tips

What to watch during practice sessions this week:

☐ Dynamics

☐ Fingering

☐ Hand Position

☐ Rhythm

☐ Other_____

_____

Teacher's Evaluation of Lesson

☐ Excellent   ☐ Very Good   ☐ Good   ☐ Satisfactory   ☐ Needs Attention

Comments: ....

....

Note from Teacher to Parent:

....

....

....

....

....

Note from Parent to Teacher:

....

....

....

....

....

What to Bring to the Next Lesson: In addition to all the music listed in the Assignment section above, bring the following materials to the next lesson: ....

....

Practice Suggestions

Assignment
For Next Lesson

Date	
Day	
Time	

Today's Lesson

Date _____

Day _____

Time _____

Method Books	New pages	Review pages
☐ Lesson Book		
☐ Theory Book		
☐ Recital/Solo Book		
☐		
☐		
Supplementary Solo, Duet & Ensemble Books		
☐		
☐		
☐		
Sheet Music Solos, Duets & Ensembles		
☐		
☐		
☐		

A check in the box is a reminder to read the Practice Suggestions on the next page.

Daily Practice Time
(in minutes)

Monday _____

Tuesday _____

Wednesday _____

Thursday _____

Friday _____

Saturday _____

Sunday _____

Practice Tips

What to watch during practice sessions this week:

☐ Dynamics

☐ Fingering

☐ Hand Position

☐ Rhythm

☐ Other _____

_____

Teacher's Evaluation of Lesson

☐ Excellent   ☐ Very Good   ☐ Good   ☐ Satisfactory   ☐ Needs Attention

Comments: ....

....

....

Note from Teacher to Parent:

....

....

....

....

....

Note from Parent to Teacher:

....

....

....

....

....

What to Bring to the Next Lesson: In addition to all the music listed in the Assignment section above, bring the following materials to the next lesson: ....

....

Practice Suggestions

Assignment

For Next Lesson

Date	
Day	
Time	

Method Books	New pages	Review pages
☐ Lesson Book		
☐ Theory Book		
☐ Recital/Solo Book		
☐		
☐		
Supplementary Solo, Duet & Ensemble Books		
☐		
☐		
☐		
Sheet Music Solos, Duets & Ensembles		
☐		
☐		
☐		

A check in the box is a reminder to read the Practice Suggestions on the next page.

Today's Lesson

Date _____

Day _____

Time _____

Daily Practice Time
(in minutes)

Monday _____

Tuesday _____

Wednesday _____

Thursday _____

Friday _____

Saturday _____

Sunday _____

Practice Tips

What to watch during practice sessions this week:

☐ Dynamics

☐ Fingering

☐ Hand Position

☐ Rhythm

☐ Other_____

_____

Teacher's Evaluation of Lesson

☐ Excellent   ☐ Very Good   ☐ Good   ☐ Satisfactory   ☐ Needs Attention

Comments: ....

....

Note from Teacher to Parent:

Note from Parent to Teacher:

What to Bring to the Next Lesson: In addition to all the music listed in the Assignment section above, bring the following materials to the next lesson:

Practice Suggestions

Assignment
For Next Lesson

Date	
Day	
Time	

Today's Lesson

Date _____

Day _____

Time _____

Method Books	New pages	Review pages
☐ Lesson Book		
☐ Theory Book		
☐ Recital/Solo Book		
☐		
☐		
Supplementary Solo, Duet & Ensemble Books		
☐		
☐		
☐		
Sheet Music Solos, Duets & Ensembles		
☐		
☐		
☐		

A check in the box is a reminder to read the Practice Suggestions on the next page.

Daily Practice Time
(in minutes)

Monday _____

Tuesday _____

Wednesday _____

Thursday _____

Friday _____

Saturday _____

Sunday _____

Practice Tips

What to watch during practice sessions this week:

☐ Dynamics

☐ Fingering

☐ Hand Position

☐ Rhythm

☐ Other_____

_____

Teacher's Evaluation of Lesson

☐ Excellent   ☐ Very Good   ☐ Good   ☐ Satisfactory   ☐ Needs Attention

Comments: ....

....

....

Note from Teacher to Parent:

....

....

....

....

....

Note from Parent to Teacher:

....

....

....

....

....

What to Bring to the Next Lesson: In addition to all the music listed in the Assignment section above, bring the following materials to the next lesson:

....

....

34

Practice Suggestions

Assignment
For Next Lesson

Date	
Day	
Time	

Date _____

Day _____

Time _____

Method Books	New pages	Review pages
☐ Lesson Book		
☐ Theory Book		
☐ Recital/Solo Book		
☐		
☐		
Supplementary Solo, Duet & Ensemble Books		
☐		
☐		
☐		
Sheet Music Solos, Duets & Ensembles		
☐		
☐		
☐		

A check in the box is a reminder to read the Practice Suggestions on the next page.

Daily Practice Time
(in minutes)

Monday _____

Tuesday _____

Wednesday _____

Thursday _____

Friday _____

Saturday _____

Sunday _____

Practice Tips

What to watch during practice sessions this week:

☐ Dynamics

☐ Fingering

☐ Hand Position

☐ Rhythm

☐ Other_____

_____

Teacher's Evaluation of Lesson

☐ Excellent   ☐ Very Good   ☐ Good   ☐ Satisfactory   ☐ Needs Attention

Comments: ....

....

Note from Teacher to Parent:

....

....

....

....

....

Note from Parent to Teacher:

....

....

....

....

....

What to Bring to the Next Lesson: In addition to all the music listed in the Assignment section above, bring the following materials to the next lesson:

....

....

Practice Suggestions

Assignment
For Next Lesson

Date	
Day	
Time	

Today's Lesson
Date _____
Day _____
Time _____

Method Books	New pages	Review pages
☐ Lesson Book		
☐ Theory Book		
☐ Recital/Solo Book		
☐		
☐		
Supplementary Solo, Duet & Ensemble Books		
☐		
☐		
☐		
Sheet Music Solos, Duets & Ensembles		
☐		
☐		
☐		

A check in the box is a reminder to read the Practice Suggestions on the next page.

Daily Practice Time
(in minutes)

Monday _____
Tuesday _____
Wednesday _____
Thursday _____
Friday _____
Saturday _____
Sunday _____

Practice Tips
What to watch during practice sessions this week:

☐ Dynamics
☐ Fingering
☐ Hand Position
☐ Rhythm
☐ Other_____
_____

Teacher's Evaluation of Lesson

☐ Excellent   ☐ Very Good   ☐ Good   ☐ Satisfactory   ☐ Needs Attention

Comments: ....

....

Note from Teacher to Parent:

....

Note from Parent to Teacher:

....

What to Bring to the Next Lesson: In addition to all the music listed in the Assignment section above, bring the following materials to the next lesson:

....

Practice Suggestions

Assignment
For Next Lesson

Date
Day
Time

Today's Lesson

Date _____

Day _____

Time _____

Method Books	New pages	Review pages
☐ Lesson Book		
☐ Theory Book		
☐ Recital/Solo Book		
☐		
☐		
Supplementary Solo, Duet & Ensemble Books		
☐		
☐		
☐		
Sheet Music Solos, Duets & Ensembles		
☐		
☐		
☐		

A check in the box is a reminder to read the Practice Suggestions on the next page.

Daily Practice Time
(in minutes)

Monday _____

Tuesday _____

Wednesday _____

Thursday _____

Friday _____

Saturday _____

Sunday _____

Practice Tips

What to watch during practice sessions this week:

☐ Dynamics

☐ Fingering

☐ Hand Position

☐ Rhythm

☐ Other_____

_____

Teacher's Evaluation of Lesson

☐ Excellent   ☐ Very Good   ☐ Good   ☐ Satisfactory   ☐ Needs Attention

Comments: ....

....

....

Note from Teacher to Parent:

....

....

....

....

....

Note from Parent to Teacher:

....

....

....

....

....

What to Bring to the Next Lesson: In addition to all the music listed in the Assignment section above, bring the following materials to the next lesson: ....

....

....

Practice Suggestions

Assignment
For Next Lesson

Date
Day
Time

Method Books	New pages	Review pages
☐ Lesson Book		
☐ Theory Book		
☐ Recital/Solo Book		
☐		
☐		
Supplementary Solo, Duet & Ensemble Books		
☐		
☐		
☐		
Sheet Music Solos, Duets & Ensembles		
☐		
☐		
☐		

A check in the box is a reminder to read the Practice Suggestions on the next page.

Daily Practice Time
(in minutes)

Monday _____

Tuesday _____

Wednesday _____

Thursday _____

Friday _____

Saturday _____

Sunday _____

Practice Tips

What to watch during practice sessions this week:

☐ Dynamics

☐ Fingering

☐ Hand Position

☐ Rhythm

☐ Other_____

_____

Teacher's Evaluation of Lesson

☐ Excellent   ☐ Very Good   ☐ Good   ☐ Satisfactory   ☐ Needs Attention

Comments: ....

....

Note from Teacher to Parent:

....

....

....

....

Note from Parent to Teacher:

....

....

....

....

What to Bring to the Next Lesson: In addition to all the music listed in the Assignment section above, bring the following materials to the next lesson: ....

....

....

Practice Suggestions

Assignment
For Next Lesson

Date
Day
Time

Today's Lesson

Date

Day

Time

Method Books	New pages	Review pages
☐ Lesson Book		
☐ Theory Book		
☐ Recital/Solo Book		
☐		
☐		
Supplementary Solo, Duet & Ensemble Books		
☐		
☐		
☐		
Sheet Music Solos, Duets & Ensembles		
☐		
☐		
☐		

A check in the box is a reminder to read the Practice Suggestions on the next page.

Daily Practice Time
(in minutes)

Monday _____

Tuesday _____

Wednesday _____

Thursday _____

Friday _____

Saturday _____

Sunday _____

Practice Tips

What to watch during
practice sessions this week:

☐ Dynamics

☐ Fingering

☐ Hand Position

☐ Rhythm

☐ Other_____

_____

Teacher's Evaluation of Lesson

☐ Excellent   ☐ Very Good   ☐ Good   ☐ Satisfactory   ☐ Needs Attention

Comments:

Note from Teacher to Parent:

Note from Parent to Teacher:

What to Bring to the Next Lesson: In addition to all the music listed in the Assignment section above, bring the following materials to the next lesson:

Practice Suggestions

Assignment
For Next Lesson

Date
Day
Time

Today's Lesson

Date _____

Day _____

Time _____

Method Books	New pages	Review pages
☐ Lesson Book		
☐ Theory Book		
☐ Recital/Solo Book		
☐		
☐		
Supplementary Solo, Duet & Ensemble Books		
☐		
☐		
☐		
Sheet Music Solos, Duets & Ensembles		
☐		
☐		
☐		

A check in the box is a reminder to read the Practice Suggestions on the next page.

Daily Practice Time
(in minutes)

Monday _____

Tuesday _____

Wednesday _____

Thursday _____

Friday _____

Saturday _____

Sunday _____

Practice Tips

What to watch during practice sessions this week:

☐ Dynamics

☐ Fingering

☐ Hand Position

☐ Rhythm

☐ Other_____

_____

Teacher's Evaluation of Lesson

☐ Excellent   ☐ Very Good   ☐ Good   ☐ Satisfactory   ☐ Needs Attention

Comments: ....

....

....

Note from Teacher to Parent:

Note from Parent to Teacher:

What to Bring to the Next Lesson: In addition to all the music listed in the Assignment section above, bring the following materials to the next lesson: ....

....

....

Practice Suggestions

Assignment
For Next Lesson

Date
Day
Time

Today's Lesson

Date

Day

Time

Method Books	New pages	Review pages
☐ Lesson Book		
☐ Theory Book		
☐ Recital/Solo Book		
☐		
☐		
Supplementary Solo, Duet & Ensemble Books		
☐		
☐		
☐		
Sheet Music Solos, Duets & Ensembles		
☐		
☐		
☐		

A check in the box is a reminder to read the Practice Suggestions on the next page.

Daily Practice Time
(in minutes)

Monday _____

Tuesday _____

Wednesday _____

Thursday _____

Friday _____

Saturday _____

Sunday _____

Practice Tips

What to watch during practice sessions this week:

☐ Dynamics

☐ Fingering

☐ Hand Position

☐ Rhythm

☐ Other_____

_____

Teacher's Evaluation of Lesson

☐ Excellent ☐ Very Good ☐ Good ☐ Satisfactory ☐ Needs Attention

Comments: ....

....

Note from Teacher to Parent:

Note from Parent to Teacher:

What to Bring to the Next Lesson: In addition to all the music listed in the Assignment section above, bring the following materials to the next lesson:

Practice Suggestions

Assignment
For Next Lesson

Date	
Day	
Time	

Method Books	New pages	Review pages
☐ Lesson Book		
☐ Theory Book		
☐ Recital/Solo Book		
☐		
☐		
Supplementary Solo, Duet & Ensemble Books		
☐		
☐		
☐		
Sheet Music Solos, Duets & Ensembles		
☐		
☐		
☐		

A check in the box is a reminder to read the Practice Suggestions on the next page.

Daily Practice Time
(in minutes)

Monday _____
Tuesday _____
Wednesday _____
Thursday _____
Friday _____
Saturday _____
Sunday _____

Practice Tips
What to watch during practice sessions this week:

☐ Dynamics
☐ Fingering
☐ Hand Position
☐ Rhythm
☐ Other_____

_____

Teacher's Evaluation of Lesson

☐ Excellent   ☐ Very Good   ☐ Good   ☐ Satisfactory   ☐ Needs Attention

Comments: ....
....
....

Note from Teacher to Parent:
....
....
....
....
....

Note from Parent to Teacher:
....
....
....
....
....

What to Bring to the Next Lesson: In addition to all the music listed in the Assignment section above, bring the following materials to the next lesson:
....
....

Practice Suggestions

Assignment
For Next Lesson

Date
Day
Time

Method Books	New pages	Review pages
☐ Lesson Book		
☐ Theory Book		
☐ Recital/Solo Book		
☐		
☐		
Supplementary Solo, Duet & Ensemble Books		
☐		
☐		
☐		
Sheet Music Solos, Duets & Ensembles		
☐		
☐		
☐		

A check in the box is a reminder to read the Practice Suggestions on the next page.

Daily Practice Time
(in minutes)

Monday _____

Tuesday _____

Wednesday _____

Thursday _____

Friday _____

Saturday _____

Sunday _____

Practice Tips

What to watch during practice sessions this week:

☐ Dynamics

☐ Fingering

☐ Hand Position

☐ Rhythm

☐ Other_____

_____

Teacher's Evaluation of Lesson

☐ Excellent   ☐ Very Good   ☐ Good   ☐ Satisfactory   ☐ Needs Attention

Comments: ....

....

....

Note from Teacher to Parent:

....

....

....

....

....

Note from Parent to Teacher:

....

....

....

....

....

What to Bring to the Next Lesson: In addition to all the music listed in the Assignment section above, bring the following materials to the next lesson:

....

....

Practice Suggestions

Assignment
For Next Lesson

Date
Day
Time

Method Books	New pages	Review pages
☐ Lesson Book		
☐ Theory Book		
☐ Recital/Solo Book		
☐		
☐		
Supplementary Solo, Duet & Ensemble Books		
☐		
☐		
☐		
Sheet Music Solos, Duets & Ensembles		
☐		
☐		
☐		

A check in the box is a reminder to read the Practice Suggestions on the next page.

Daily Practice Time
(in minutes)

Monday _____

Tuesday _____

Wednesday _____

Thursday _____

Friday _____

Saturday _____

Sunday _____

Practice Tips
What to watch during practice sessions this week:

☐ Dynamics

☐ Fingering

☐ Hand Position

☐ Rhythm

☐ Other _____

_____

Teacher's Evaluation of Lesson

☐ Excellent   ☐ Very Good   ☐ Good   ☐ Satisfactory   ☐ Needs Attention

Comments: ....

....

....

Note from Teacher to Parent:

....

....

....

....

Note from Parent to Teacher:

....

....

....

....

What to Bring to the Next Lesson: In addition to all the music listed in the Assignment section above, bring the following materials to the next lesson:

....

....

Practice Suggestions

Assignment
For Next Lesson

Date	
Day	
Time	

Date _____
Day _____
Time _____

Method Books	New pages	Review pages
☐ Lesson Book		
☐ Theory Book		
☐ Recital/Solo Book		
☐		
☐		
Supplementary Solo, Duet & Ensemble Books		
☐		
☐		
☐		
Sheet Music Solos, Duets & Ensembles		
☐		
☐		
☐		

A check in the box is a reminder to read the Practice Suggestions on the next page.

Daily Practice Time
(in minutes)

Monday _____
Tuesday _____
Wednesday _____
Thursday _____
Friday _____
Saturday _____
Sunday _____

Practice Tips
What to watch during practice sessions this week:
☐ Dynamics
☐ Fingering
☐ Hand Position
☐ Rhythm
☐ Other_____
_____

Teacher's Evaluation of Lesson
☐ Excellent   ☐ Very Good   ☐ Good   ☐ Satisfactory   ☐ Needs Attention

Comments: ....
....
....

Note from Teacher to Parent:
....
....
....
....
....

Note from Parent to Teacher:
....
....
....
....
....

What to Bring to the Next Lesson: In addition to all the music listed in the Assignment section above, bring the following materials to the next lesson: ....
....
....

Practice Suggestions

Assignment
For Next Lesson

Date	
Day	
Time	

Method Books	New pages	Review pages
☐ Lesson Book		
☐ Theory Book		
☐ Recital/Solo Book		
☐		
☐		
Supplementary Solo, Duet & Ensemble Books		
☐		
☐		
☐		
Sheet Music Solos, Duets & Ensembles		
☐		
☐		
☐		

A check in the box is a reminder to read the Practice Suggestions on the next page.

Daily Practice Time
(in minutes)

Monday _____
Tuesday _____
Wednesday _____
Thursday _____
Friday _____
Saturday _____
Sunday _____

Practice Tips
What to watch during practice sessions this week:

☐ Dynamics
☐ Fingering
☐ Hand Position
☐ Rhythm
☐ Other_____
_____

Teacher's Evaluation of Lesson

☐ Excellent   ☐ Very Good   ☐ Good   ☐ Satisfactory   ☐ Needs Attention

Comments:
....
....
....

Note from Teacher to Parent:

....
....
....
....
....

Note from Parent to Teacher:

....
....
....
....
....

What to Bring to the Next Lesson: In addition to all the music listed in the Assignment section above, bring the following materials to the next lesson:

....
....

Practice Suggestions

Assignment
For Next Lesson

Date
Day
Time

Method Books	New pages	Review pages
☐ Lesson Book		
☐ Theory Book		
☐ Recital/Solo Book		
☐		
☐		
Supplementary Solo, Duet & Ensemble Books		
☐		
☐		
☐		
Sheet Music Solos, Duets & Ensembles		
☐		
☐		
☐		

A check in the box is a reminder to read the Practice Suggestions on the next page.

Daily Practice Time
(in minutes)

Monday _____

Tuesday _____

Wednesday _____

Thursday _____

Friday _____

Saturday _____

Sunday _____

Practice Tips
What to watch during practice sessions this week:

☐ Dynamics

☐ Fingering

☐ Hand Position

☐ Rhythm

☐ Other_____

Teacher's Evaluation of Lesson

☐ Excellent   ☐ Very Good   ☐ Good   ☐ Satisfactory   ☐ Needs Attention

Comments: ....

....

....

Note from Teacher to Parent:

....

....

....

....

....

Note from Parent to Teacher:

....

....

....

....

....

What to Bring to the Next Lesson: In addition to all the music listed in the Assignment section above, bring the following materials to the next lesson: ....

....

....

Practice Suggestions

Assignment
For Next Lesson

Date	
Day	
Time	

Today's Lesson
Date _____
Day _____
Time _____

Method Books	New pages	Review pages
☐ Lesson Book		
☐ Theory Book		
☐ Recital/Solo Book		
☐		
☐		
Supplementary Solo, Duet & Ensemble Books		
☐		
☐		
☐		
Sheet Music Solos, Duets & Ensembles		
☐		
☐		
☐		

A check in the box is a reminder to read the Practice Suggestions on the next page.

Daily Practice Time
(in minutes)

Monday _____
Tuesday _____
Wednesday _____
Thursday _____
Friday _____
Saturday _____
Sunday _____

Practice Tips
What to watch during practice sessions this week:

☐ Dynamics
☐ Fingering
☐ Hand Position
☐ Rhythm
☐ Other_____
_____

Teacher's Evaluation of Lesson

☐ Excellent   ☐ Very Good   ☐ Good   ☐ Satisfactory   ☐ Needs Attention

Comments: ....
....

Note from Teacher to Parent:

....
....
....
....
....

Note from Parent to Teacher:

....
....
....
....
....

What to Bring to the Next Lesson: In addition to all the music listed in the Assignment section above, bring the following materials to the next lesson:

....
....

Practice Suggestions

Assignment
For Next Lesson

Date
Day
Time

Today's Lesson
Date _____
Day _____
Time _____

Method Books	New pages	Review pages
☐ Lesson Book		
☐ Theory Book		
☐ Recital/Solo Book		
☐		
☐		
Supplementary Solo, Duet & Ensemble Books		
☐		
☐		
☐		
Sheet Music Solos, Duets & Ensembles		
☐		
☐		
☐		

A check in the box is a reminder to read the Practice Suggestions on the next page.

Daily Practice Time
(in minutes)

Monday _____
Tuesday _____
Wednesday _____
Thursday _____
Friday _____
Saturday _____
Sunday _____

Practice Tips
What to watch during practice sessions this week:

☐ Dynamics
☐ Fingering
☐ Hand Position
☐ Rhythm
☐ Other_____
_____

Teacher's Evaluation of Lesson

☐ Excellent   ☐ Very Good   ☐ Good   ☐ Satisfactory   ☐ Needs Attention

Comments: ....
....

Note from Teacher to Parent:
....
....
....
....
....

Note from Parent to Teacher:
....
....
....
....
....

What to Bring to the Next Lesson: In addition to all the music listed in the Assignment section above, bring the following materials to the next lesson:
....
....

Practice Suggestions

Assignment
For Next Lesson

Date	
Day	
Time	

Date _____

Day _____

Time _____

Method Books	New pages	Review pages
☐ Lesson Book		
☐ Theory Book		
☐ Recital/Solo Book		
☐		
☐		
Supplementary Solo, Duet & Ensemble Books		
☐		
☐		
☐		
Sheet Music Solos, Duets & Ensembles		
☐		
☐		
☐		

A check in the box is a reminder to read the Practice Suggestions on the next page.

Daily Practice Time
(in minutes)

Monday _____

Tuesday _____

Wednesday _____

Thursday _____

Friday _____

Saturday _____

Sunday _____

Practice Tips

What to watch during practice sessions this week:

☐ Dynamics

☐ Fingering

☐ Hand Position

☐ Rhythm

☐ Other_____

_____

Teacher's Evaluation of Lesson

☐ Excellent   ☐ Very Good   ☐ Good   ☐ Satisfactory   ☐ Needs Attention

Comments: ....

....

....

Note from Teacher to Parent:

....

....

....

....

....

Note from Parent to Teacher:

....

....

....

....

....

What to Bring to the Next Lesson: In addition to all the music listed in the Assignment section above, bring the following materials to the next lesson:

....

....

Practice Suggestions

Music I Have Memorized

Music Books & Pieces I Have Studied

Music Books

....
....
....
....
....
....
....
....
....
....
....

Sheet Music Solos, Duets and Ensembles

....
....
....
....
....
....
....
....
....
....
....

Music I Have Performed

Piece	Date	Event
....	....	....
....	....	....
....	....	....
....	....	....
....	....	....
....	....	....
....	....	....
....	....	....
....	....	....
....	....	....
....	....	....
....	....	....
....	....	....
....	....	....
....	....	....
....	....	....
....	....	....
....	....	....
....	....	....
....	....	....
....	....	....
....	....	....
....	....	....
....	....	....

Music I Have Borrowed from My Teacher

Music	Date Borrowed	Date Returned
....	....	....
....	....	....
....	....	....
....	....	....
....	....	....
....	....	....
....	....	....
....	....	....
....	....	....
....	....	....
....	....	....
....	....	....
....	....	....
....	....	....
....	....	....
....	....	....
....	....	....
....	....	....
....	....	....
....	....	....
....	....	....
....	....	....
....	....	....

Dictionary of Music Terms

Accent (>) ....placed over or under a note that gets special emphasis. Play the note louder.

Accidental ....a sharp or flat not given in the key signature.

Adagio ....slowly.

Allegro ....quickly, happily.

Andante ....moving along (at walking speed).

A tempo ....resume original speed.

Crescendo (◁) ....gradually louder.

Da Capo al Fine (D.C. al Fine) ....repeat from the beginning and play to the Fine (end).

Diminuendo (▷) ....gradually softer.

Dynamic signs ....signs showing how loud or soft to play.

Fermata (⌒) ....indicates that a note should be held longer than its true value.

Fine...the end.

First ending (⌐1.   ⌐) ....the measures under the bracket are played the 1st time only.

Flat sign (♭)..lowers a note one half step. Play the next key to the left.

Forte (𝑓) ....loud.

Half step ....the distance from one key to the very next one, with no key between.

Harmonic interval ....the interval between two tones sounded together.

Incomplete measure................................a measure at the beginning of a piece with fewer counts than shown in the time signatures. The missing counts are found in the last measure.

Interval ....the difference in pitch (highness or lowness) between two tones.

Key signature...the number of sharps or flats in any key—written at the beginning of each line.

Legato...smoothly connected. Usually indicated by a slur over or under the notes.

Major scale ....a series of 8 notes made of two tetrachords joined by a whole step.

Melodic interval.......................................the interval between two tones sounded separately.

Mezzo forte (𝑚𝑓).....................................moderately loud.